YOU'RE A GRAND OLD FLAG

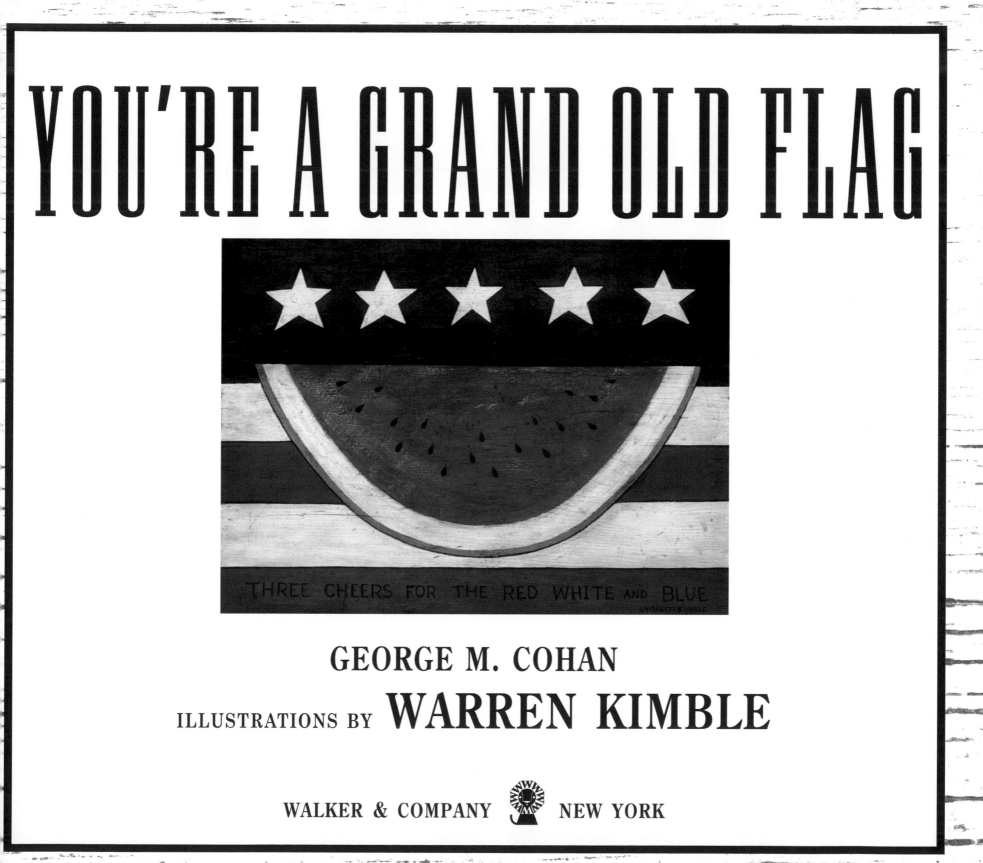

THREE CHEERS FOR THE RED WHITE AND BLUE

GEORGE M. COHAN
ILLUSTRATIONS BY WARREN KIMBLE

WALKER & COMPANY NEW YORK

AMERICAN SOFA PAINTING

First published in the United States of America in 2007 by
Walker Publishing Company, Inc.
Distributed to the trade by Holtzbrinck Publishers

For information about permission to reproduce selections
from this book, write to Permissions, Walker & Company,
104 Fifth Avenue, New York, New York 10011

Library of Congress Cataloging-in-Publication Data
Cohan, George M. (George Michael), 1878–1942.
You're a grand old flag / [illustrated] by Warren Kimble.
    p.   cm.
Summary: An illustrated version of the song honoring the American flag.
ISBN-13: 978-0-8027-9575-5 • ISBN-10: 0-8027-9575-7 (hardcover)
ISBN-13: 978-0-8027-9576-2 • ISBN-10: 0-8027-9576-5 (reinforced bdg.)
[1. Flags—United States—Songs and music. 2. Patriotic music. 3. Songs.]
I. Kimble, Warren, ill. II. Title. III. Title: You are a grand old flag.
PZ8.3.C655You 2007   782.42—dc22 [E]   2006035328

The illustrations for this book were created
using acrylic Winsor & Newton paint on distressed wood.

Book design by E. Friedman

Visit Walker & Company's Web site at www.walkeryoungreaders.com

Printed in Malaysia
2 4 6 8 10 9 7 5 3 1

All papers used by Walker & Company are natural, recyclable products
made from wood grown in well-managed forests. The manufacturing processes
conform to the environmental regulations of the country of origin.

AMERICA

REN KIMBLE

You're
a grand
old flag,

You're
a high
flying
flag

©WARREN KIMBLE

And forever
in peace
may you wave.

You're
the emblem
of

The land I love.

© WARREN KIMBLE

The home of the free and the brave.

Ev'ry heart beats true

'Neath
the Red, White, and Blue,

© WARREN KIMBLE

Where there's never
a boast or brag.

Should
auld acquaintance
be forgot,

Keep your eye
on the grand old flag.

SONG NOTES

"You're a Grand Old Flag" was written by George M. Cohan for his show GEORGE WASHINGTON, JR., which premiered in 1906. It was immediately popular and was the first song from a musical to sell more than a million copies of sheet music. Cohan wrote the song after he met a Civil War veteran who was holding a carefully folded but ragged old flag. It is said that he saw Cohan looking at the flag and said, "She's a grand old rag." Cohan thought that was a great line and originally used it as his song title. But so many people objected to his calling the flag a "rag" that he had to change the song title to "You're a Grand Old Flag."

FLAG FACTS

In May of 1776, Betsy Ross is believed to have sewn the first American flag. Many people think, however, that the first flag was designed by Francis Hopkinson. The first official American flag was established by the Continental Congress on June 14, 1777. It was made of thirteen stripes, alternating red and white, along with thirteen white stars against a blue field. Flag Day is now celebrated every June 14 to commemorate this act.

Between 1777 and 1960, the flag went through many changes to reflect our growing nation. Today's flag is made up of thirteen horizontal stripes: seven red stripes alternating with six white stripes, to represent the thirteen original colonies. There are also fifty white stars against a dark blue background to represent each state in the union. The red in our flag symbolizes hardiness and valor; the white represents purity and innocence; and the flag's blue stands for vigilance, perseverance, and justice.

You're a Grand Old Flag

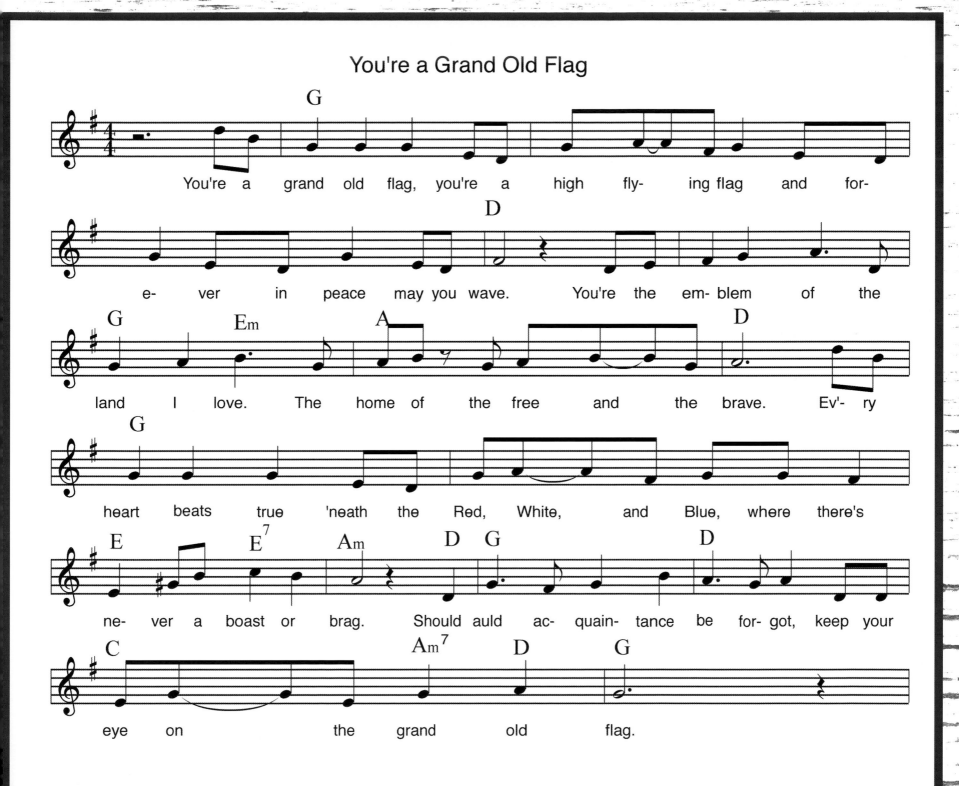